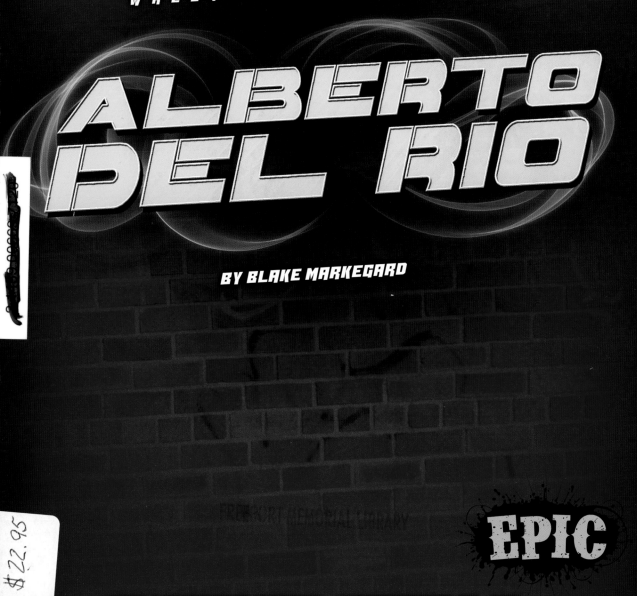

ALBERTO DEL RIO

BY BLAKE MARKEGARD

EPIC

BELLWETHER MEDIA • MINNEAPOLIS, MN

EPIC BOOKS are no ordinary books. They burst with intense action, high-speed heroics, and shadows of the unknown. Are you ready for an Epic adventure?

This edition first published in 2015 by Bellwether Media, Inc.

No part of this publication may be reproduced in whole or in part without written permission of the publisher. For information regarding permission, write to Bellwether Media, Inc., Attention: Permissions Department, 5357 Penn Avenue South, Minneapolis, MN 55419.

Library of Congress Cataloging-in-Publication Data

Markegard, Blake.
  Alberto Del Rio / by Blake Markegard.
      pages cm. – (Epic: Wrestling Superstars)
  Includes bibliographical references and index.
  Summary: "Engaging images accompany information about Alberto Del Rio. The combination of high-interest subject matter and light text is intended for students in grades 2 through 7"– Provided by publisher.
  ISBN 978-1-62617-139-8 (hardcover : alk. paper)
  1. Rio, Alberto del, 1977–Juvenile literature. 2. Wrestlers–United States–Biography–Juvenile literature. I. Title.
  GV1196.R55M37 2014
  796.812092–dc23
  [B]
                              2014002069

Printed in the United States of America, North Mankato, MN.

TABLE OF CONTENTS

WARNING!

The wrestling moves used in this book are performed by professionals.
Do not attempt to reenact any of the moves performed in this book.

THE DEBUT

Alberto Del Rio drives to the ring in a fancy car. This is just his **debut**. But he already acts like a star.

ROLLS-ROYCE PHANTOM

★

The 1965 classic Cobra
is Del Rio's favorite car.
He likes its power.

REY MYSTERIO

Del Rio battles Rey Mysterio inside the ring. Eventually, he pulls out his Cross Armbreaker. This hold forces Mysterio to **tap out**. Del Rio wins!

WHO IS ALBERTO DEL RIO?

Alberto Del Rio is a WWE superstar nicknamed The Mexican **Aristocrat**. Fans know him for being **arrogant** inside and outside the ring.

★

The Essence of Excellence is another nickname for Del Rio.

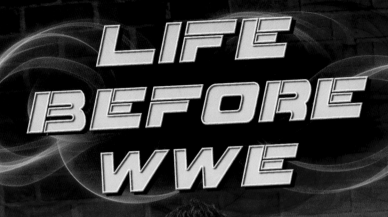

LIFE BEFORE WWE

DOS CARAS

Del Rio believes he was **destined** for greatness. He was born into a family of Mexican wrestlers. His father is the famous **luchador** Dos Caras.

ALMOST ANYTHING GOES

★

Del Rio also fought as a mixed martial artist in Japan. Mixed martial artists use wrestling, boxing, and karate moves.

He started out as a **Greco-Roman wrestler** in Mexico. In time, Del Rio moved on to **lucha libre**. He wore a mask and called himself Dos Caras, Jr.

DOS CARAS, JR.

A WWE SUPERSTAR

STAR PROFILE

WRESTLING NAME: Alberto Del Rio

REAL NAME: Alberto Rodríguez

BIRTHDATE: May 25, 1977

HOMETOWN: San Luis Potosí, Mexico

HEIGHT: 6 feet, 5 inches (2 meters)

WEIGHT: 239 pounds (108 kilograms)

WWE DEBUT: 2010

FINISHING MOVE: Cross Armbreaker

In 2010, Del Rio joined WWE. He traded his mask for a silk scarf. It took him less than a year to win a championship.

Del Rio has won several major **titles** since his debut. Crowds have booed him along the way. Fans see him as a **heel**.

WINNING MOVES

The Cross Armbreaker has sealed many of Del Rio's victories. This **finishing move** traps an opponent on the mat. Then Del Rio pulls on his arm. Soon the opponent gives up because of the pain.

CROSS
ARMBREAKER

The Enzuigiri is another signature move. Del Rio charges at an opponent. Then he jumps and kicks the opponent in the back of the head. What a blow!

ENZUIGIRI

FITTING NAME

★

Enzuigiri means "to chop the back of the head" in Japanese.

GLOSSARY

aristocrat—a person who is born into a rich and powerful family

arrogant—being too proud of oneself

debut—first official appearance

destined—meant for something

finishing move—a wrestling move that finishes off an opponent

Greco-Roman wrestler—a wrestler who fights without tripping, tackling, or using certain holds on opponents

heel—a wrestler viewed as a villain

lucha libre—professional wrestling in Mexico; lucha libre is known for high-flying moves.

luchador—a professional wrestler in Mexico; a luchador wears a mask and performs high-flying moves.

signature move—a move that a wrestler is famous for performing

tap out—to lose by giving up

titles—championships

TO LEARN MORE

At the Library

Black, Jake. *WWE General Manager's Handbook.* New York, N.Y.: Grosset & Dunlap, 2012.

Markegard, Blake. *Rey Mysterio.* Minneapolis, Minn.: Bellwether Media, 2015.

West, Tracey. *Race to the Rumble.* New York, N.Y.: Grosset & Dunlap, 2011.

On the Web

Learning more about Alberto Del Rio is as easy as 1, 2, 3.

1. Go to www.factsurfer.com.

2. Enter "Alberto Del Rio" into the search box.

3. Click the "Surf" button and you will see a list of related web sites.

With factsurfer.com, finding more information is just a click away.

INDEX